The Pianist's Chord Manual

ERNEST LUBIN

Amsco Publications
New York/London/Sydney

International Standard Book Number: 0.8256.2150.X
Library of Congress Card Catalog Number: 70-170118

Exclusive Distributors:
Music Sales Corporation
225 Park Avenue South, New York, NY 10003
Music Sales Limited
8/9 Frith Street, London W1V 5TZ England
Music Sales Pty. Limited
120 Rothschild Street, Rosebery, Sydney, NSW 2018, Australia

Printed in the United States of America by
Vicks Lithograph and Printing Corporation

Contents

The Instrument

Have you ever stopped to think what a remarkable instrument the piano is? If you play a wind instrument, such as the flute or the trumpet, for example, you can produce only one melodic line at a time. Or if you have a stringed instrument, such as the violin or the guitar, then the presence of a few strings together will allow for some possibility of harmonic effects, but under considerable limitations.

With the piano, however, you have at your command an instrument that can produce any kind of harmony that you wish in an almost infinite variety of forms, while you can still play the melody along with it yourself. You have at your disposal a range of tones from the lowest to the highest, as well as a level of dynamics from the softest to the loudest, and all of this can be held together with the pedal, which itself lends an added variety of musical coloration.

Even if you are a beginner, you can soon learn to harmonize the melodies you play—and if you wish to do that, then this book is designed to help you on a simple enough level for you to work out on your own. The main body of the book consists of a table of the chords that are most commonly used and indicated in popular sheet music. Even if you can't read music, you can glance at the type of chord indicated above the guitar tablature, and by referring to that particular chord in our table of chords, you can find a suitable harmony for your melody.

Of course, you are better off if you can read music a little, and we shall try to help you there too, at least on an elementary level, since fortunately, it is not at all difficult to pick up.

Reading Notes

You had better know the names of the notes first, and to introduce you to them, we have appended a diagram of a portion of the piano keyboard, with the names of the notes indicated on them.

A B C D E F G A B C D E F G A B C

As you can see, the names of the notes range from A to G, and then start all over again. Perhaps the easiest way to learn to identify the notes is by learning them in terms of the black notes of the keyboard, which are grouped, as you will notice, in twos and threes. The name of the white note between the group of two black notes is D. If you can remember that, then you can figure out any other note from there. Thus, if you go down step by step from any D on the piano, you will come to C, then next to B, and then to A. Contrariwise, if you go up from D, you will come to E, then F, and then G.

After that you start again at the higher octave. The *octave,* by the way, is simply a term that refers to a distance of eight notes, after which the patterns of notes repeat themselves.

Now let us get down to cases. See if you can find the note C at the piano—that is, the note just below D, or just below any group of two black notes at the piano. There are eight C's on the keyboard. Now look for the C in the middle of the piano, nearest the name of the piano-maker. That particular C is known as *middle C,* and we shall use that as a handy reference guide in our illustrations.

One reason we have chosen the note, C, by the way, is that it is the easiest note on which to build a scale, since it doesn't require the use of any black notes.

Scales

You will have to learn to use the black notes too before long, and they really aren't difficult—but for the time being, let us stick with the white ones, and build a scale on C, going up on all the white notes until we come to the C an octave above. Here are the notes you have played on our keyboard diagram:

And here they are in standard musical notation:

You have just played the *major* scale on C, the most commonly used type of scale in music.

The other scale commonly used as well as the major scale is the *minor* scale, and it differs from the major scale in that two of its tones are lowered. If you would like to play the minor scale on C, start as you did before on middle C, but when you come to the third note of the scale, the E, play the black note just below it instead. This note is called E *flat*. Now continue with F and G, and when you come to the sixth note of the scale, the A, substitute for it instead the black note just below it, or A flat, and then finish with B and C. Now you have learned the minor scale as well as the major scale!

By the way, get acquainted with the musical symbol for a flat, written as follows: ♭

Here is the scale of minor written out in terms of the piano keyboard:

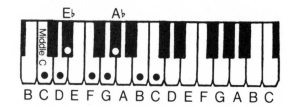

And here it is in musical notation:

Sharps And Flats

You have just learned that the black note just *below* any white note is a flat. If you're wondering what a sharp is, it's very simple—just play the black note above any white note, and you've played a sharp! Thus the black note just above C is called C *sharp;* here it is on our diagram (the musical sign for a sharp is #):

This note also happens to be a D flat too, and any black note can be either a flat or a sharp, depending on how it is approached.

Chords

Now let us apply some of our knowledge about the notes of the keyboard to constructing chords, which is, after all, what this book is all about!

Since you will usually play the melody in your right hand, and accompany yourself with chords in your left hand, we shall now move down the keyboard a little to the C an octave below middle C.

Find that C on the piano—here it is in tablature:

Now let us see about building a chord above it. The simplest way of constructing a chord is in *thirds*—that is, you skip the second note just above the note you are starting with, and go to the third note above it. That interval is known simply as a third. If you have started with C, you will skip to the E above it for the next note of your chord. Then skip to the third above that for the next note of your chord, G, and you will now have a complete chord of three notes, C, E and G.

Here they are in our tablature notation— play them together as a chord:

Since it's good to learn as much as you can about musical notation here's that same chord written in musical notation, as it would appear in a piece of music.

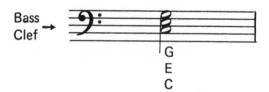

Playing with the left hand below middle C, we have used the *bass* clef, which is the clef normally used for the left hand in the lower part of the keyboard. The clef used for the right hand is called the *treble* clef or G clef. Here is the chord of C in the G clef, going up from middle C: (You can play this with the right hand.)

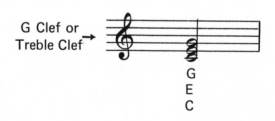

Some New Chords

Now that you have learned the C major chord, one of the simplest and most basic chords in music, let us see if we can vary it slightly to get a new chord and a new harmonic color. If you will take the middle note, E, of your C major chord, and substitute for it the black note just below it, you will have a chord of C, E♭ and G, which is another very commonly used chord, the chord of C minor. Here it is in musical notation and in tablature :

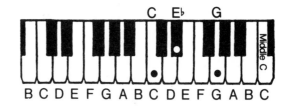

Play it, and listen to the sound of it as compared to the C major chord.

Would you like another variation? Well, play the top note flat too—that will give you a chord of C, E♭ and G♭. That's another chord you will come across sometimes—not quite as frequently as the C major and C minor chords, but you should know it too. It is called the *diminished* chord.

Here it is in notation and in tablature —try it:

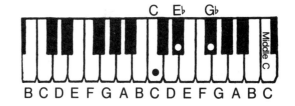

Now that you have learned three very useful chords, practice them separately and together, and see if you can recognize the distinctive tone color of each one of them.

Here are the three of them together in musical notation; we'll skip the tablature this time.

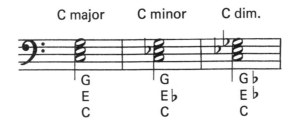

Seventh Chords

Now if you know these chords fairly well, you may be ready for something a little more complicated; let us see if we can learn to use chords of four notes. They are a little more difficult, but not much—and when you harmonize melodies, you will often need them.

Play the C major chord again, consisting of the notes C, E and G—but this time include a fourth note with it, the note B♭ above G. Here it is in tablature and notation:

This is an extremely important chord, known as the *dominant seventh* chord on C.

If you'd like another variation of harmonic color, play the same chord, but lower the E into E♭ as follows:

This is a chord of the minor seventh—a very beautiful one!

Here is still another variation—lower the G as well to a G♭; now you have a half-diminished chord:

These chords all belong to the family of *seventh* chords, so called because the distance between their outer notes is a seventh, or seven notes, counting the starting note of C in the bass as the first note.

Here is one last variation of the seventh chord. If you will take the last chord you had, and lower the top note of B♭ one note further, to the A just below it, you will have what is known as the diminished seventh chord, one of the most frequently used chords in music:

How do you like the sound of that one? It is the kind of chord that was particularly favored by the pianists in the old silent movies during the exciting moments when the villain was either stealing away the heroine or being furiously chased by the hero. It has a very dramatic and individual character of its own.*

*Don't be disconcerted in case you noticed that the distance between the two outer notes from C to A is only six notes, or apparently a sixth; it's still really a seventh chord, for the A is technically a B double flat. But that's a little advanced for now, so don't worry about it as long as you can play the chord correctly.

Chords Of The Sixth

Now let us finish our preliminary work by trying a few chords of the sixth. Here is a simple sixth chord, consisting of the notes C, E and A.

Here is another, known as the *six-four* chord, made up of the notes C, F and A.

And here is still another, known as the chord of the *added sixth,* the notes of this are C, E, G and A.

There are an almost infinite number of ways that you can vary these chords, and use them in different manners and styles. It might take years of study of the art of harmony to really understand them all—but at least many of them aren't too difficult for you to play.

Here is a little *progression*—the term used for a series of chords, one going into another—that you might like to try just for practice.

Here is another progression, this one a little more *chromatic*—that is, with more sharps and flats. Try your luck with it if you'd like something a little more difficult:

F major
2nd Inversion

A♭ Chord

You have begun with a six-four chord on C (that is, an F major chord in the second inversion) and ended with the major chord of A flat, in which the lowest note is doubled at the octave. Perhaps you might like to experiment with other chords yourself to see what interesting and beautiful progressions you can devise.

Inversions

By now you should be able to tackle the main body of the book, which is simply a table listing most of the chords you are likely to find in popular music. This is primarily a reference work, so keep them handy when you wish to accompany the melodies you play at the piano. Perhaps in time you may get to know many of these chords by heart, and you may get to read music more easily, so that you can learn more about the piano and about harmony. But in the meantime, this manual may be a help and a stepping stone.

One last point before you start using this manual. You should be aware that you have a considerable amount of leeway in using any of these chords. You can use them in any octave or in any position, dividing them between the hands if you wish, or playing them in single notes, one after another. (This kind of pattern is called an "arpeggio".) You can even switch the octave between any of the notes of a chord, and the chord will still have the same basic function. Thus when you play the very first chord of the manual, the A major chord consisting of A, C# and E, you may find the position rather low, and a little harsh in that register. On the other hand, if you took it up an entire octave, it might be too high to accompany your melody. Thus you can adapt your original position of the chord (or the *fundamental* position, when the three notes of the chord are in thirds), by placing the lowest note in the higher octave, while keeping the other two notes as they are. This will give you a chord with C# as the lowest note, followed by E and A (or if you'd like to know its technical name, the first inversion of the A major chord). Now if you wish you can repeat the process once more, taking the low C# of the first inversion and raising it an octave, giving you a chord of E, A and C#, or the second inversion of the A major chord. For your convenience, we have written out each of the major and minor chords in every key in the fundamental position and in both the first and second inversions. You can use any form of them that you wish, as long as it sounds good, fits into your hand, and follows easily from the previous chord.

Now take out your music, and see how it works. Good luck!

Chord Manual

The following pages list the most commonly used chords based on each of the twelve musical notes, beginning with A and going up to A♭.

The following chords are included, both in piano tablature and musical notation:

I. The major chord and its inversions
II. The minor chord and its inversions
III. The dominant seventh chord
IV. The minor seventh chord
V. The diminished seventh chord
VI. The chord of the added sixth

Remember that the sixth chords will appear only as inversions of the simple major and minor chords.

For example, a sixth chord with C as its lowest note will appear either under *A* (C, E and A being the *first inversion* of the A minor chord), or under *F,* (C, F and A being the *second inversion* of the F major chord).

Although the inversions of the *seventh chords* are not written out here, these can be worked out by using the same method we used in forming inversions of the three-note major and minor chords; that is, by taking the lowest note of the chord up an octave without changing the remaining notes.

Thus the inversions of the dominant seventh chord built on A would appear as follows:

Fundamental   1st   2nd   3rd
position   Inversion Inversion Inversion

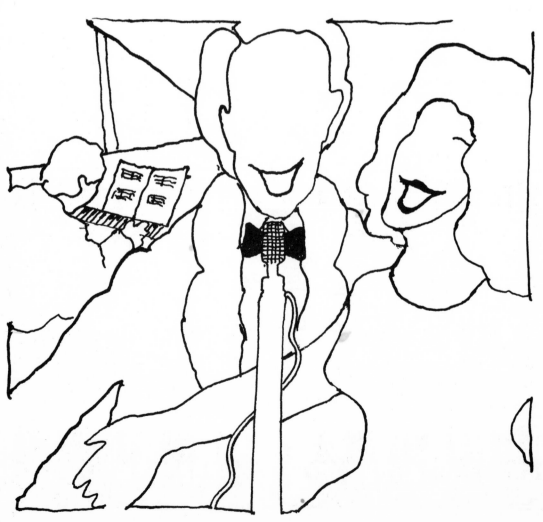

Chords On A

A MAJOR CHORD

A MINOR CHORD

DOMINANT SEVENTH ON A

MINOR SEVENTH ON A

DIMINISHED SEVENTH ON A

CHORD OF THE ADDED SIXTH ON A

Chords On Bb

Bb MAJOR CHORD

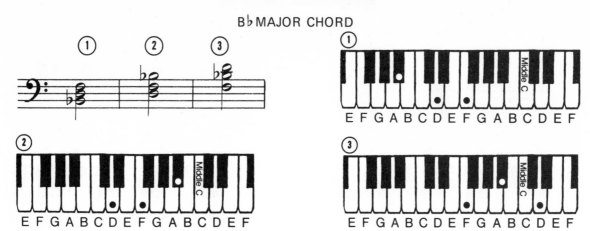

Bb MINOR CHORD

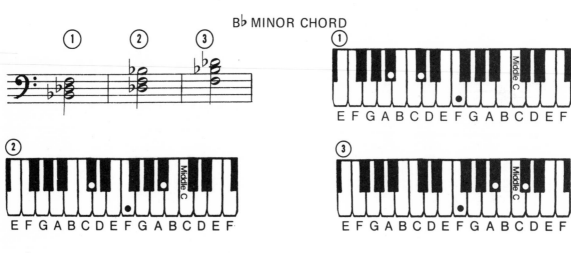

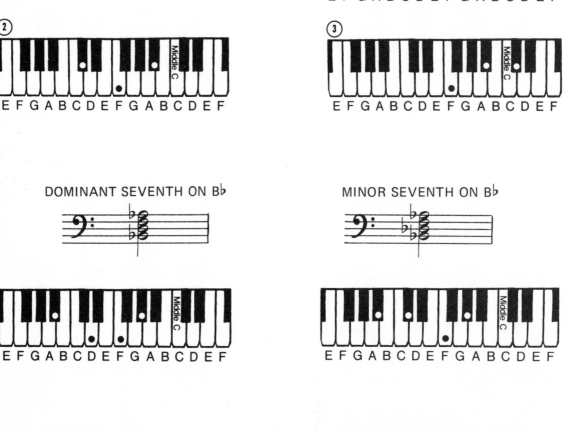

DOMINANT SEVENTH ON Bb

MINOR SEVENTH ON Bb

DIMINISHED SEVENTH ON Bb

CHORD OF THE ADDED SIXTH ON Bb

Chords On B

B MAJOR CHORD

B MINOR CHORD

DOMINANT SEVENTH ON B

MINOR SEVENTH ON B

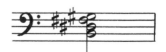

DIMINISHED SEVENTH ON B

CHORD OF THE ADDED SIXTH ON B

Chords On C

C MAJOR CHORD

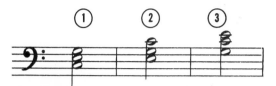

C MINOR CHORD

DOMINANT SEVENTH ON C

MINOR SEVENTH ON C

DIMINISHED SEVENTH ON C

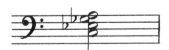

CHORD OF THE ADDED SIXTH ON C

Chords On Db (or C#)

Db MAJOR CHORD (or C# MAJOR CHORD)

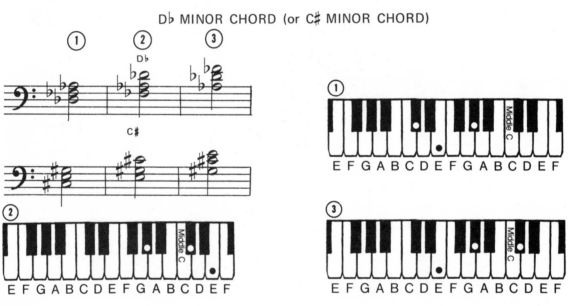

Db MINOR CHORD (or C# MINOR CHORD)

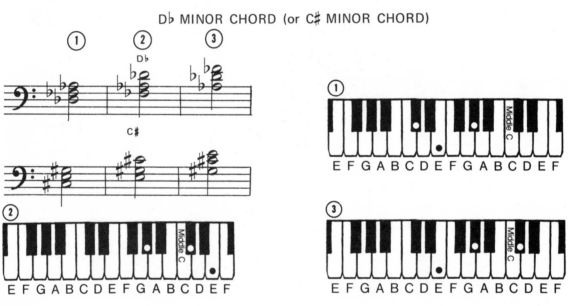

DOMINANT SEVENTH ON Db (or C#)   MINOR SEVENTH ON Db (or C#)

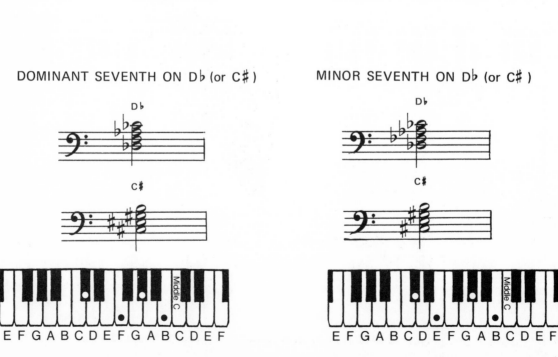

DIMINISHED SEVENTH ON D♭ (or C♯)　　　CHORD OF THE ADDED
　　　　　　　　　　　　　　　　　　　　SIXTH ON D♭ (or C♯)

Chords On D

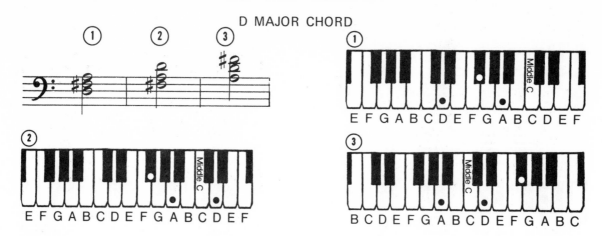

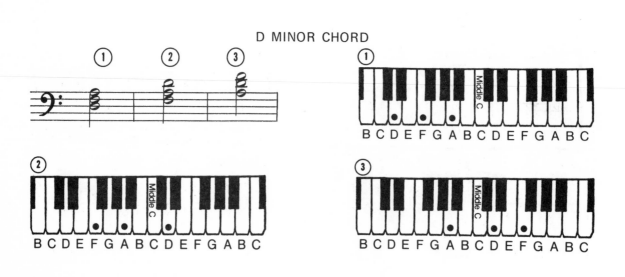

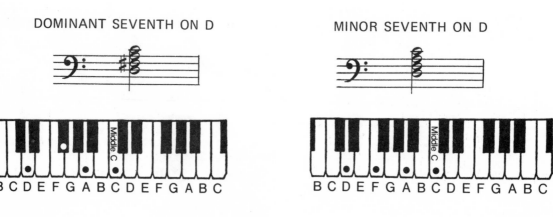

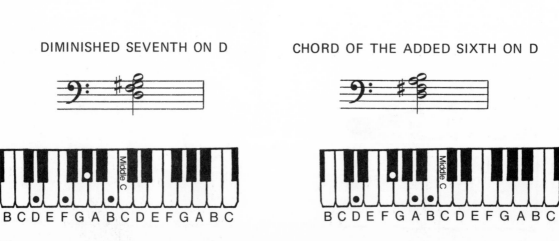

Chords On E♭

E♭ MAJOR CHORD

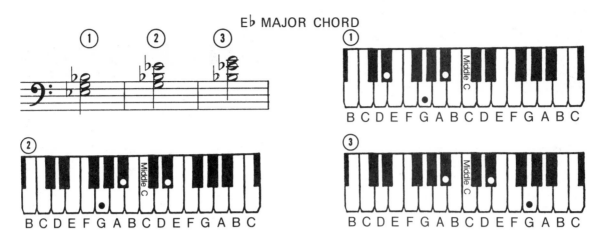

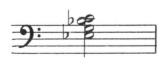

E♭ MINOR CHORD

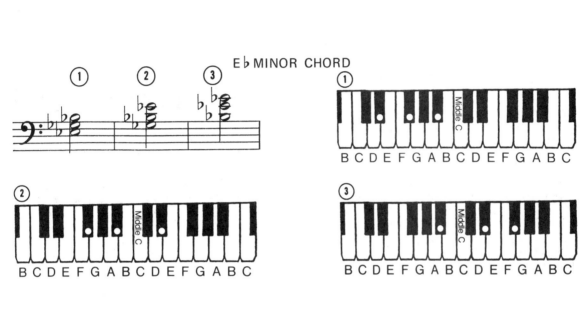

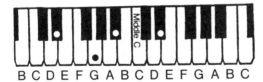

DOMINANT SEVENTH CHORD ON E♭

MINOR SEVENTH CHORD ON E♭

DIMINISHED SEVENTH CHORD ON E♭

CHORD OF THE ADDED SIXTH ON E♭

23

Chords On E

E MAJOR CHORD

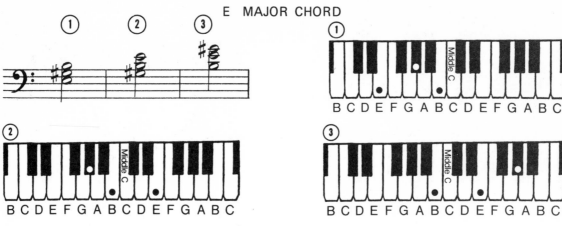

E MINOR CHORD

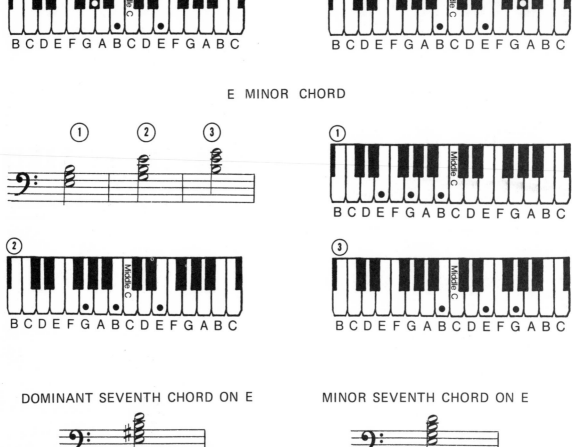

DOMINANT SEVENTH CHORD ON E

MINOR SEVENTH CHORD ON E

DIMINISHED SEVENTH CHORD ON E

CHORD OF THE ADDED SIXTH ON E

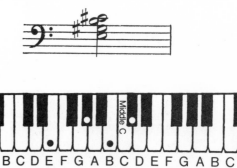

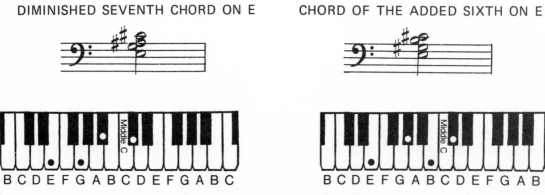

Chords On F

F MAJOR CHORD

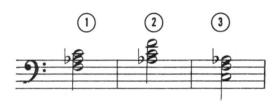

F MINOR CHORD

DOMINANT SEVENTH CHORD ON F

MINOR SEVENTH CHORD ON F

DIMINISHED SEVENTH CHORD ON F

CHORD OF THE ADDED SIXTH ON F

25

Chords On F# (or Gb)

F# MAJOR CHORD (or Gb MAJOR CHORD)

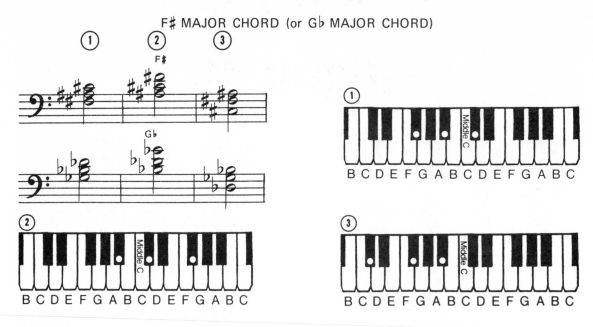

F# MINOR CHORD

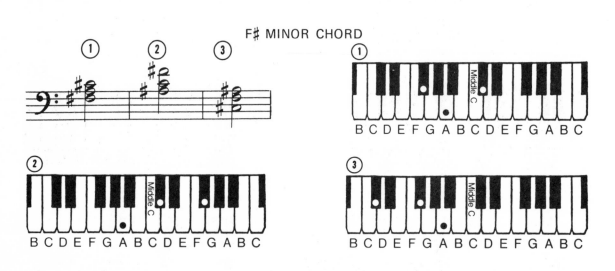

DOMINANT SEVENTH CHORD ON F# (or Gb)

MINOR SEVENTH CHORD ON F♯

B C D E F G A B C D E F G A B C

DIMINISHED SEVENTH CHORD ON F♯ (or G♭)

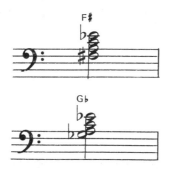

CHORD OF THE ADDED SIXTH ON F♯ (or G♭)

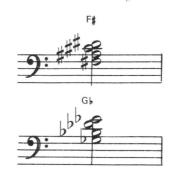

B C D E F G A B C D E F G A B C

B C D E F G A B C D E F G A B C

27

Chords On G

G MAJOR CHORD

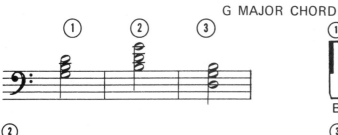

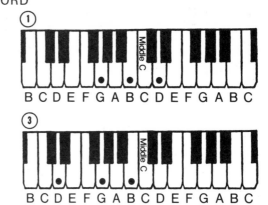

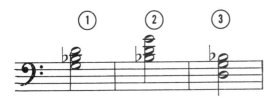

G MINOR CHORD

DOMINANT SEVENTH CHORD ON G

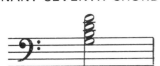

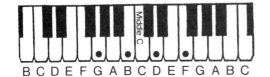

MINOR SEVENTH CHORD ON G

DIMINISHED SEVENTH CHORD ON G

CHORD OF THE ADDED SIXTH ON G

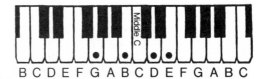

29

Chords On Ab

Ab MAJOR CHORD

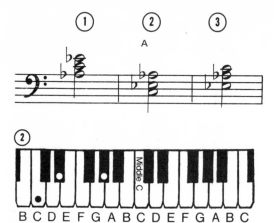

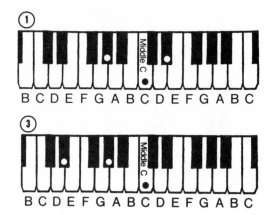

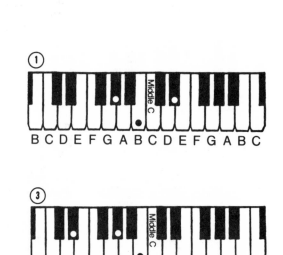

Ab MINOR CHORD (or G# MINOR CHORD)

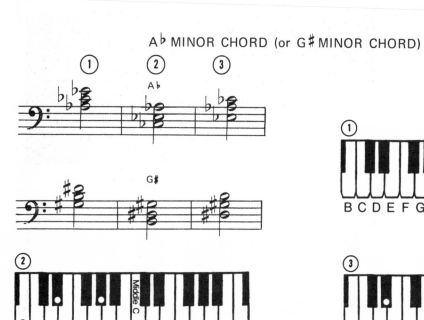

DOMINANT SEVENTH CHORD ON Ab

CHORD OF THE ADDED SIXTH ON Ab

30

DIMINISHED SEVENTH
CHORD ON A♭ (or G♯)

MINOR SEVENTH
CHORD ON A♭ (or G♯)

BCDEFGABCDEFGABC

BCDEFGABCDEFGABC

Some Basic Principles Of Harmony

In the preceding chord manual we have treated each of the individual chords as separate entities, but in reality they begin to acquire meaning only when they are used in context with other chords—just as words begin to acquire meaning only when they are used with other words to form phrases and sentences.

You have noticed, for example, that the C major, F major and G major chords are the chords on the first degree of the scale in the keys of C, F and G. But in the key of C major these chords are also the chords built on the first, the fourth and the fifth degrees of the scale of C—and it is in this context that they are used to harmonize melodies in the key of C. These three chords, in fact, are so important and basic to our system of harmony that they are sufficient to harmonize, at least in a simple form, any standard or traditional melody. The chords built on the other degrees of the scale are important too—but they are used primarily to provide additional variety and harmonic color around these three chords—the one chord, the four chord and the five chord, to give them their technical names. (Incidentally, these chords have additional names of their own that are very frequently used; the I chord is also known as the *tonic* chord, the IV chord as the *sub-dominant* chord, and the V chord as the *dominant* chord.)

Let us see now how we can apply these three chords to the harmonization of a simple melody. Let us try *Oh, Susannah,* which you undoubtedly know.

OH, SUSANNAH

In choosing the harmonies, remember that you do not have to harmonize every single note; in fact, such a harmonization would be unbearably complicated and fussy. Rather you will find that the important notes of the melody will suggest an appropriate harmony, and generally speaking, one, or occasionally two chords to a measure will be quite sufficient. In other words, try to choose a chord whose notes are importantly represented in the melody. If you play or sing the opening two bars of *Oh, Susannah* you will see that they more or less outline the chord of C.

Thus they suggest the use of the C major chord, and if you try playing the C major chord along with these two bars you will find that it fits very well:

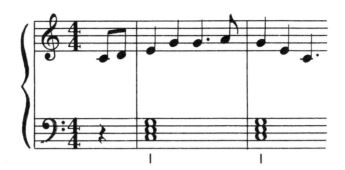

Actually you won't have to change the chord until the fourth bar of the tune, when the note D would not fit with the I chord any longer, but (as one of the notes that comprise the G major or V chord) would suggest the V chord for use at this point. Now let us try these opening four bars, and see how they sound with the harmonization that we have suggested:

During the opening three bars, the momentary appearance of notes not forming part of the C major chord (indicated by asterisks) does not affect the use of the C major chord in the harmonization. They are only *passing* tones (as in the case of the D, which quickly passes from the notes C and E of the C major chord), or *neighboring* tones (as in the case of the A, which leaves the note G for a moment, only to return to it almost immediately).

However, the note D which fills the fourth measure, is clearly much too important a note of the melody to be a mere passing tone or neighboring tone, and we must harmonize it with its own chord, the G major chord, or the V chord in C, of which it is a part.

The next four measures of the melody are very much like the first, except that we will have to end the musical phrase with the I chord. Therefore we will harmonize the two quarter note D's just before it with the V chord to provide a little variety. Here then are the first eight measures of *Oh, Susannah* harmonized simply with the I and V chords in the key of C.

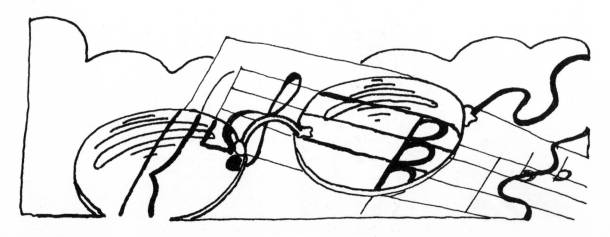

Now let us go further and see what chord we will need to harmonize the continuation of the melody; here are the ninth and tenth measures of our tune:

These notes, F and A, are obviously not a part of either the I chord (C major—C, E and G) or the V chord (G major—G, B and D), but a moment's glance will suggest the IV chord of C; that is, the F major chord consisting of F, A and C. The F and A both belong to the IV chord—let us try it:

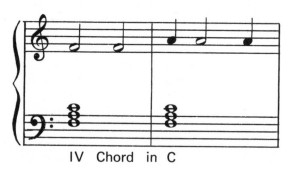

IV Chord in C

Perfect! Now we have begun to learn how to harmonize a melody, and from here to the end of the entire melody you will see that the I, IV and V chords will serve very well to provide a simple and suitable harmonization. Try to harmonize it to the end by yourself, and then compare it with this version

Oh, Susannah—1st Version

Of course, this harmonization is quite simple, not to say elementary, and you may wish to look for ways to make it more varied and interesting. One possibility is to take the V chord that we have used and transform it into the V7 chord, or dominant seventh chord which we have discussed on page 10.*

*Incidentally, you could if you wished also make seventh chords out of the I chord and the IV chord in C, but the seventh formed on these chords is a sharper and slightly harsher interval (a major seventh instead of a minor seventh, if you want to be technical) and it is used much less frequently than the seventh built on the V chord.

Now let us see how *Oh, Susannah—2nd Version* sounds if we used the dominant seventh chord instead of the simple dominant chord:

Oh, Susannah—2nd Version

This is already an improvement over our very simple first harmonization! If you would like to vary it still more, you can alter the chords by using the *inversions* that we have discussed on page 13—that is, you can change the position of any chord by choosing a different note to serve as its lowest note or bass. Here then is a third and still further improved harmonization of *Oh, Susannah* into which we have introduced a few inversions:

Oh, Susannah—3rd Version

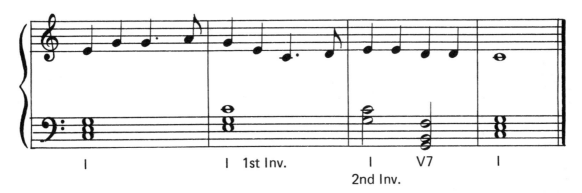

V7 1st Inv.   I   I 1st Inv.   I   V7
          2nd Inv.

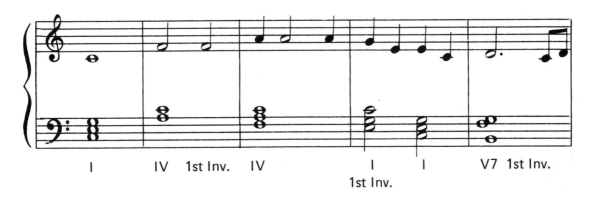

I   IV 1st Inv.   IV   I   I   V7 1st Inv.
                                                        1st Inv.

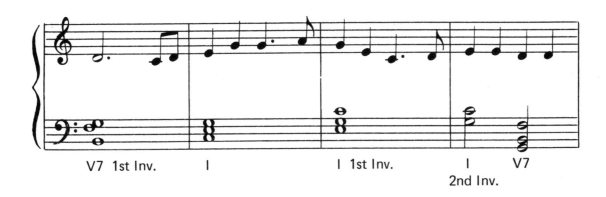

I   I 1st Inv.   I   V7   I
          2nd Inv.

Of course, we can harmonize *Oh, Susannah* just as easily in any one of the other major keys (there are twelve in all, built on each of the notes, white and black, within the octave). Let us try a fourth version in the key of F, exactly as we had it before, but now *transposed**
four notes higher:

*When we switch music from one key to another we are transposing it, but when we move from one key to another, as for example, starting in C and then going to the key of G or any other key, then we are *modulating*. Both these terms, "transposing" and "modulating" are used very often, and you should know what they mean.

Oh, Susannah—4th Version

Later on we will use the chords built on the other notes of the scale as well as the I, IV and V chords—and they provide very necessary and beautiful effects of variety. But they are a little more advanced, and in your first attempts at harmonization, you will find it easier to work with these basic chords of I, IV and V for a while.

Arpeggios

Once you have begun to feel at home with the chords we have been discussing, you may be ready to experiment with other ways of using these chords. For example, you can play the notes of the chord one after another instead of all together. In this case you will be playing an *arpeggio* (named after the Italian word for harp) a most useful and effective way of varying your chords.

Thus the C major chord in its fundamental position can be played with its three notes one after another as follows:

The four notes of the dominant seventh chord on C could equally well be played this way:

When you are playing a piece in three quarters time you will find that an arpeggio pattern of three notes will just fill out the three quarter beats of the measure. But in this case when you come to a four note chord such as a dominant seventh or a diminished seventh, then you will find that the simplest way to fit the four notes of the chord into a measure of three quarters time is to leave out one of them.

Here as a typical example is a harmonization in the key of F of the opening bars of that charming melody by Richard Rodgers, *Falling in Love with Love:*

FALLING IN LOVE WITH LOVE

V7

You will notice that when we came to the dominant seventh chord on C in measures five to eight of our example, we left out the note G in the left hand arpeggio—the reason being that the note G appears in the melody at this point, and so in a way is already represented in the harmony. If the melody had gone instead to E, then we would probably have omitted the note E in the accompaniment and used G instead as follows:

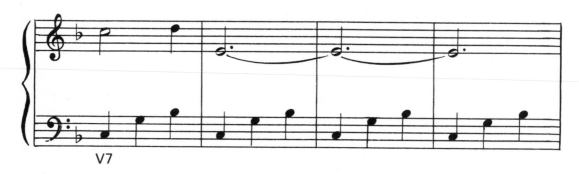

Falling in Love with Love
By: Richard Rodgers, Lorenz Hart
Copyright © 1938 by Chappell & Co., Inc.
Copyright renewed. Used by permission of Chappell & Co., Inc.

When you are playing a piece in four quarters time, then of course you will be able to fill out the measure with all the notes that make up such a four note chord as the dominant seventh. By now when you come to a three note chord, you may very possibly find it expedient to add an extra note to it by "doubling" one of the notes of the chord—that is, repeating it at another octave. Here is an arpeggio progression of the C dominant seventh chord to a simple three note F major chord, using this device:

C dominant 7   F Major

As you can see, the note F of the F major chord is repeated at the higher octave to finish the measure. Here are some other patterns that can be used in fitting three note chords into a four beat measure:

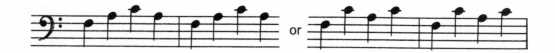

or

40

Another manner of forming an arpeggio accompaniment—and one that is used extremely often—is to take the lowest note of the chord as the first beat of the measure, and then combine the other notes of the chord together and repeat them for the remaining beats of the measure. Here is how *Falling in Love with Love* would begin with this type of accompaniment:

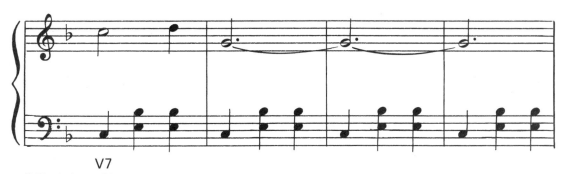

Falling in Love with Love
By: Richard Rodgers, Lorenz Hart
Copyright © 1938 by Chappell & Co., Inc.
Copyright renewed. Used by permission of Chappell & Co., Inc.

This accompaniment pattern provides a particularly strong accent on the first beat of the measure, and with its strongly rhythmic character is most helpful when you wish to emphasize the dance-like quality of the music you are playing. Here are a few ways in which this type of accompaniment can be used in four quarters time:

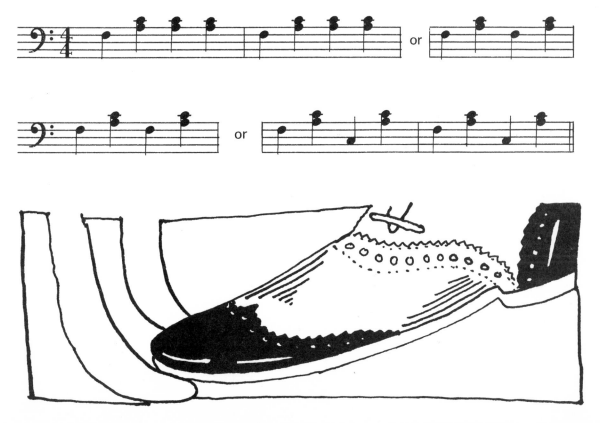

Here is how *Oh, Susannah* would sound with this last type of accompaniment, which provides a strong, swinging beat:

Oh, Susannah—5th Version

(left hand always staccato)

One great advantage of an arpeggio accompaniment is that it frees you from the limitations of what a single hand can reach. If you play all the notes of a chord together in one hand you will not find it easy to stretch more than an octave, but when you play them one after another, you can easily spread them out to a much greater range. Thus a simple C major chord can be varied in arpeggio patterns as follows, affording you a greater sonority than would be possible otherwise:

If you would like to see with what skill and artistry these arpeggio patterns can be used, then look into the arpeggio figurations in the compositions of Chopin, Liszt and other great composers for the piano. Here are two ways that Chopin has varied the simple I chord in the left hand accompaniments to his nocturnes. (For convenience, we have put them both into the key of C, and simplified the $\frac{6}{8}$ and $\frac{12}{8}$ notation into three quarters time).

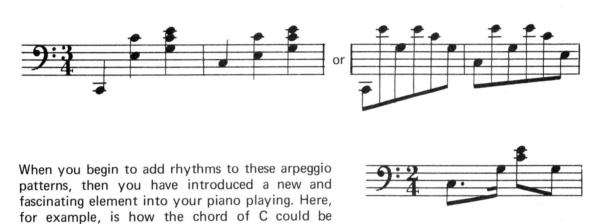

When you begin to add rhythms to these arpeggio patterns, then you have introduced a new and fascinating element into your piano playing. Here, for example, is how the chord of C could be adapted to suggest the rhythm of a tango:

And here is a bolero rhythm for the left hand:

When you begin to consider the variations that are possible by introducing jazz rhythms into your accompaniments, then you have added still another dimension to your playing. These jazz rhythms make particular use of the device of "syncopation" that is, of anticipating the rhythm before its normal beat and thus displacing the accent. If you have a good ear for jazz, perhaps you may be able to pick up some of these syncopated rhythms by instinct. Their musical notation is a little complicated, but if you would like to explore them further, you might find it helpful to pick up such books as Win Stormen's *Popular Piano Self-Taught* published by the Amsco Music Publishing Company, or Denes Agay's *The Joy of Jazz,* published by Yorktown Music Press; both are excellent introductions to the subject.

The Pedal

With these more extended forms of the chords that we have been discussing, you will find it helpful—and in fact, almost necessary—to add the pedal, and perhaps it might be wise at this point to take a moment to discuss its use. The most important pedal, and in fact, the only one that you will need, is the one at the right, which is sometimes referred to as the loud pedal in contrast to the one at the left, the soft pedal, which reduces the volume of the piano. But the function of this pedal is not to make the tone louder, but rather to sustain any tone that you have played, even after you are no longer holding it down.

Thus to take one of the extended forms of the arpeggio that we have discussed—this measure of accompaniment consists only of separate notes when you don't use the pedal—but when you add the pedal, it is as though you were still holding down the lowest note, even though you had to let it go in order to reach the upper notes—and the actual effect suggests the illusion that you are playing with two hands, as follows:

In addition there is an added resonance due to the fact that all the dampers of the piano have been released, which allows all the notes of the C major chord throughout the entire range of the piano to sound "sympathetically" along with the notes you have played—an effect which is not easy to explain, and which may not even be noticed as such, but which lends a very real added sonority to the piano. No wonder that the pedal has been called "the soul of the piano"!

However, when you use the pedal, you must be careful to change it every time you change the chord. Otherwise the different chords will all run together to create a confused and muddy sound which you will wish to avoid.

You can notice this very simply if you play the following C major and G major chords, holding the pedal continuously:

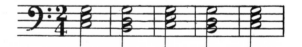

To play this passage musically, you will have to change the pedal each time you change the chord.

When you have become accustomed to using the pedal and wish to try a little finesse, then see if you can wait to raise your foot from the pedal until you have just played the new chord, and then put it back down immediately. This may require a little attention to co-ordination at first, but when you have learned to do it (and it will come more or less automatically after a while) then you will find that it is the most satisfactory way of using the pedal, for it avoids any break in the sound as you change the chord.

The Predecessors Of The Piano

You may be interested in noting that the pedal as we know it did not exist in the keyboard instruments that preceded the piano, such as the harpsichord and the clavichord.* They were beautiful instruments in their own way, and have enjoyed a considerable revival in recent years, largely due to the efforts of Wanda Landowska whose recordings of the keyboard music of the early composers on the harpsichord are wonderful monuments of musical artistry. But their resources were extremely limited in certain ways as compared to the piano.*

The tone of the harpsichord was produced by plucking the strings, and that of the clvichord by rubbing the strings. The piano, on the other hand, strikes the strings with hammers, enabling it to produce gradations of loud and soft by the pressure of the fingers. This, incidentally, is the source of the name of the pianoforte (to give it its full title) which in Italian means "soft-loud", and which constituted its most striking novelty when it first appeared. The piano was first invented by Cristofori in the 1720's, but it did not replace the harpsichord in general use until the latter part of the eighteenth century, or roughly speaking, the time of Haydn and Mozart. When you hear the music of Bach and earlier composers played on the piano, it is well to remember that you are actually hearing a transcription of music that sounded quite different on the instrument for which it was originally intended.

Needless to say, the piano has enjoyed a great development in terms of range, power and mechanical perfection since its early days. If you are curious about its construction, here is a diagram of the action of a modern grand piano.

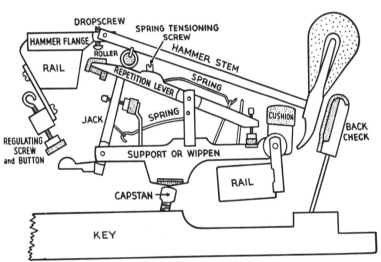

Illustration from: Piano, Pianists and Sonics *by G.A. Briggs Used by permission of author.*

It would appear, in terms of the mechanism of the instrument, that once a piano key has been struck, it can make no difference in the resulting tone, whether it has been struck by the hand of a fine pianist, or by an iron rod, or even by an umbrella handle, and in fact the famous scientist, Sir James Jeans once engaged in a long and heated discussion with the English piano pedagogue, Tobias Matthay in support of this proposition. From a scientific point of view it would seem hard to question his position. And yet all the same, it is amazing how the touch of one musician can differ from another. Some pianists have a more brilliant, and some a more sensitive touch, and certainly it is not easy to explain how certain pianists acquire the magical gift of making the instrument sing. But if you play the piano enough, there is no doubt that in time you can develop your own recognizable style and touch.

*The larger harpsichords did sometimes have a pedal keyboard, which produced a scale in the bass like the pedal keyboard of the organ.

The Metronome

Sometimes you may notice that the tempo at the beginning of a piece is indicated by a metronome mark, such as ♩ = 60. This means that your metronome—a mechanical instrument that beats the time—must be set to the figure 60, and that each quarter note will be counted at that speed. A tempo of 60, incidentally, would be one beat to a second, for the metronome figure is set to the number of counts in a minute. A tempo of 120 would be twice as fast, of 120 beats to a minute, and the other numbers are scaled in proportion.

The metronome was first created by a very clever inventor named Maelzel who lived in the early years of the nineteenth century. Beethoven was interested in the metronome and became a friend of Maelzel; once he wrote a humorous composition for him imitating the clicking sound of the metronome, which he later developed into the second movement of his *Eighth Symphony*. Maelzel's original instrument was a simple thing with a clock-like mechanism, but nowadays you can get electrical forms of the instrument which give you a choice of a flashing light as well as a ticking sound.

Perhaps you may be interested in getting a metronome to help you keep time at the piano. Musical rhythms are built around a steady beat, which is maintained at approximately the same speed for an entire piece unless indicated otherwise. Of course you cannot play with the rigidity of a metronome—but often it is helpful at a certain stage in accustoming you to count steadily.

Hand Position

If you have observed the hand position of good pianists at concerts, over television, or in photographs, you will have noticed that there is a certain amount of flexibility and variation between the hand position of one pianist and another. But generally speaking, you will get the best results if you keep your fingers curved, with the wrist fairly low and the knuckles at the highest point of your hand position. And be sure to keep the fingers close to the keys even when they are not playing a note. Try particularly to avoid the two most common errors of beginners at the piano; don't let the fingers fall flat on the keys, and on the other hand, don't let them fly in the air when they're not in use.

Avoid this:

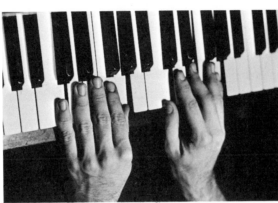

fingers flat

And avoid this:

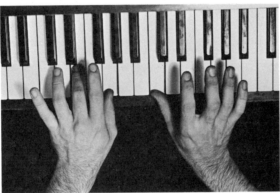

fingers in the air

But aim at this:

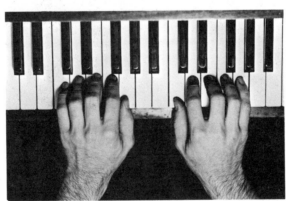

fingers curved with the tips just above the keys

And just as important as your hand position, make sure that you are seated comfortably before you start to play. Your piano chair or bench should be far enough away from the piano to allow you freedom of movement without crowding, and it should be high enough so that you never have to reach up to the keyboard.

But perhaps the best advice is that which Rachmaninoff gave a pupil who asked him, "Shall I sit high and play low, or sit low and play high?", to which Rachmaninoff replied, "Sit comfortably and play well."

Jot down your ideas in these quality manuscript books.

THE TABLATURE WRITING BOOK

Suitable for bass, guitar, banjo, or any other folk instrument. Printed on quality 6-line perforated paper. The <u>only</u> music writing book especially designed for tablature.

Order No. OK63305
ISBN: 0.8256.0187.8
$4.95/£3.95

THE PROFESSIONAL MUSIC MANUSCRIPT BOOK

Perforated 12 stave sheets of finest quality manuscript paper... plus a dictionary of musical terms, instrument ranges and transpositions, chord reference chart and common musical usages and notation.

Order No. AM36427
ISBN: 0.7119.0490.1
$4.95/£3.95

MANUSCRIPT PAPER

Over 80 12-line durable tour-out sheets, printed on both sides. This is a straight-forward, informative format book, explaining notation, note values, rests, time signatures, sharps and flats, musical terms, a chord reference chart and a guide to instrument ranges and transcription.

Order No. AM40486
ISBN: 0.8256.2117.8
$4.95/£3.95

MUSIC WRITING BOOK

High quality music writing paper is in perforated sheets, perfect for individual assignments. Includes a complete dictionary of musical terms, chord reference chart, instrument ranges and transpositions, common musical usages and notation.

Order No. AM40494
U.S. ISBN: 0.8256.2118.6
U.K. ISBN: 0.7119.0294.1
$3.95/£3.50